G000068519

Every Day Matters

2023 Diary

A Year of Inspiration for the
Mind, Body and Spirit

Created by
Jess Sharp
as seen on Instagram
@jessrachelsharp

WATKINS
Sharing Wisdom Since 1893

Every Day Matters 2023 Diary

First published in UK and USA in 2022 by
Watkins, an imprint of Watkins Media Limited
Unit 11, Shepperton House
89–93 Shepperton Road
London N1 3DF

enquiries@watkinspublishing.com

Designed by Watkins Media Limited

Commissioning Editor: Anya Hayes
Assistant Editor: Brittany Willis
Illustrator and Author: Jess Sharp
Designer: Kieryn Tyler

Desk Diary ISBN: 978-178678-660-9
Pocket Diary ISBN: 978-178678-661-6

Printed in China

Signs of the Zodiac:

♒	Aquarius	January 20 – February 17
♓	Pisces	February 19 – March 19
♈	Aries	March 20 – April 19
♉	Taurus	April 20 – May 20
♊	Gemini	May 21 – June 20
♋	Cancer	June 21 – July 21
♌	Leo	July 22 – August 22
♍	Virgo	August 23 – September 21
♎	Libra	September 22 – October 22
♏	Scorpio	October 23 – November 21
♐	Sagittarius	November 22 – December 20
♑	Capricorn	December 21 – January 19

Phases of the Moon:

● New moon
☽ First quarter
○ Full moon
☾ Last quarter

Abbreviations:

BCE: Before Common Era (equivalent of BC)
CE: Common Era (equivalent of AD)
UK: United Kingdom
SCO: Scotland
NIR: Northern Ireland
ROI: Republic of Ireland
CAN: Canada
USA: United States of America
NZ: New Zealand
AUS: Australia
ACT: Australian Capital Territory
NSW: New South Wales
NT: Northern Territory
QLD: Queensland
SA: South Australia
TAS: Tasmania
VIC: Victoria
WA: Western Australia

Publisher's Notes:

All dates relating to the zodiac signs and the
phases of the moon are based on Greenwich
Mean Time (GMT).

All North American holiday dates are based
on Eastern Standard Time (EST).

Jewish and Islamic holidays begin at sundown
on the date given. Islamic holidays may vary by
a day or two, as the Islamic calendar is based on
a combination of actual sightings of the moon
and astronomical calculations.

Note on Public Holidays:

Dates were correct at the time of going to press.

2022

JANUARY
M	TU	W	TH	F	SA	SU
					1	2
3	4	5	6	7	8	9
10	11	12	13	14	15	16
17	18	19	20	21	22	23
24	25	26	27	28	29	30
31						

FEBRUARY
M	TU	W	TH	F	SA	SU
	1	2	3	4	5	6
7	8	9	10	11	12	13
14	15	16	17	18	19	20
21	22	23	24	25	26	27
28						

MARCH
M	TU	W	TH	F	SA	SU
	1	2	3	4	5	6
7	8	9	10	11	12	13
14	15	16	17	18	19	20
21	22	23	24	25	26	27
28	29	30	31			

APRIL
M	TU	W	TH	F	SA	SU
				1	2	3
4	5	6	7	8	9	10
11	12	13	14	15	16	17
18	19	20	21	22	23	24
25	26	27	28	29	30	

MAY
M	TU	W	TH	F	SA	SU
						1
2	3	4	5	6	7	8
9	10	11	12	13	14	15
16	17	18	19	20	21	22
23	24	25	26	27	28	29
30	31					

JUNE
M	TU	W	TH	F	SA	SU
		1	2	3	4	5
6	7	8	9	10	11	12
13	14	15	16	17	18	19
20	21	22	23	24	25	26
27	28	29	30			

JULY
M	TU	W	TH	F	SA	SU
				1	2	3
4	5	6	7	8	9	10
11	12	13	14	15	16	17
18	19	20	21	22	23	24
25	26	27	28	29	30	31

AUGUST
M	TU	W	TH	F	SA	SU
1	2	3	4	5	6	7
8	9	10	11	12	13	14
15	16	17	18	19	20	21
22	23	24	25	26	27	28
29	30	31				

SEPTEMBER
M	TU	W	TH	F	SA	SU
			1	2	3	4
5	6	7	8	9	10	11
12	13	14	15	16	17	18
19	20	21	22	23	24	25
26	27	28	29	30		

OCTOBER
M	TU	W	TH	F	SA	SU
					1	2
3	4	5	6	7	8	9
10	11	12	13	14	15	16
17	18	19	20	21	22	23
24	25	26	27	28	29	30
31						

NOVEMBER
M	TU	W	TH	F	SA	SU
	1	2	3	4	5	6
7	8	9	10	11	12	13
14	15	16	17	18	19	20
21	22	23	24	25	26	27
28	29	30				

DECEMBER
M	TU	W	TH	F	SA	SU
			1	2	3	4
5	6	7	8	9	10	11
12	13	14	15	16	17	18
19	20	21	22	23	24	25
26	27	28	29	30	31	

2023

JANUARY
M	TU	W	TH	F	SA	SU
						1
2	3	4	5	6	7	8
9	10	11	12	13	14	15
16	17	18	19	20	21	22
23	24	25	26	27	28	29
30	31					

FEBRUARY
M	TU	W	TH	F	SA	SU
		1	2	3	4	5
6	7	8	9	10	11	12
13	14	15	16	17	18	19
20	21	22	23	24	25	26
27	28					

MARCH
M	TU	W	TH	F	SA	SU
		1	2	3	4	5
6	7	8	9	10	11	12
13	14	15	16	17	18	19
20	21	22	23	24	25	26
27	28	29	30	31		

APRIL
M	TU	W	TH	F	SA	SU
					1	2
3	4	5	6	7	8	9
10	11	12	13	14	15	16
17	18	19	20	21	22	23
24	25	26	27	28	29	30

MAY
M	TU	W	TH	F	SA	SU
1	2	3	4	5	6	7
8	9	10	11	12	13	14
15	16	17	18	19	20	21
22	23	24	25	26	27	28
29	30	31				

JUNE
M	TU	W	TH	F	SA	SU
			1	2	3	4
5	6	7	8	9	10	11
12	13	14	15	16	17	18
19	20	21	22	23	24	25
26	27	28	29	30		

JULY
M	TU	W	TH	F	SA	SU
					1	2
3	4	5	6	7	8	9
10	11	12	13	14	15	16
17	18	19	20	21	22	23
24	25	26	27	28	29	30
31						

AUGUST
M	TU	W	TH	F	SA	SU
	1	2	3	4	5	6
7	8	9	10	11	12	13
14	15	16	17	18	19	20
21	22	23	24	25	26	27
28	29	30	31			

SEPTEMBER
M	TU	W	TH	F	SA	SU
				1	2	3
4	5	6	7	8	9	10
11	12	13	14	15	16	17
18	19	20	21	22	23	24
25	26	27	28	29	30	

OCTOBER
M	TU	W	TH	F	SA	SU
						1
2	3	4	5	6	7	8
9	10	11	12	13	14	15
16	17	18	19	20	21	22
23	24	25	26	27	28	29
30	31					

NOVEMBER
M	TU	W	TH	F	SA	SU
		1	2	3	4	5
6	7	8	9	10	11	12
13	14	15	16	17	18	19
20	21	22	23	24	25	26
27	28	29	30			

DECEMBER
M	TU	W	TH	F	SA	SU
				1	2	3
4	5	6	7	8	9	10
11	12	13	14	15	16	17
18	19	20	21	22	23	24
25	26	27	28	29	30	31

2024

JANUARY
M	TU	W	TH	F	SA	SU
1	2	3	4	5	6	7
8	9	10	11	12	13	14
15	16	17	18	19	20	21
22	23	24	25	26	27	28
29	30	31				

FEBRUARY
M	TU	W	TH	F	SA	SU
			1	2	3	4
5	6	7	8	9	10	11
12	13	14	15	16	17	18
19	20	21	22	23	24	25
26	27	28	29			

MARCH
M	TU	W	TH	F	SA	SU
				1	2	3
4	5	6	7	8	9	10
11	12	13	14	15	16	17
18	19	20	21	22	23	24
25	26	27	28	29	30	31

APRIL
M	TU	W	TH	F	SA	SU
1	2	3	4	5	6	7
8	9	10	11	12	13	14
15	16	17	18	19	20	21
22	23	24	25	26	27	28
29	30					

MAY
M	TU	W	TH	F	SA	SU
		1	2	3	4	5
6	7	8	9	10	11	12
13	14	15	16	17	18	19
20	21	22	23	24	25	26
27	28	29	30	31		

JUNE
M	TU	W	TH	F	SA	SU
					1	2
3	4	5	6	7	8	9
10	11	12	13	14	15	16
17	18	19	20	21	22	23
24	25	26	27	28	29	30

JULY
M	TU	W	TH	F	SA	SU
1	2	3	4	5	6	7
8	9	10	11	12	13	14
15	16	17	18	19	20	21
22	23	24	25	26	27	28
29	30	31				

AUGUST
M	TU	W	TH	F	SA	SU
			1	2	3	4
5	6	7	8	9	10	11
12	13	14	15	16	17	18
19	20	21	22	23	24	25
26	27	28	29	30	31	

SEPTEMBER
M	TU	W	TH	F	SA	SU
						1
2	3	4	5	6	7	8
9	10	11	12	13	14	15
16	17	18	19	20	21	22
23	24	25	26	27	28	29
30						

OCTOBER
M	TU	W	TH	F	SA	SU
	1	2	3	4	5	6
7	8	9	10	11	12	13
14	15	16	17	18	19	20
21	22	23	24	25	26	27
28	29	30	31			

NOVEMBER
M	TU	W	TH	F	SA	SU
				1	2	3
4	5	6	7	8	9	10
11	12	13	14	15	16	17
18	19	20	21	22	23	24
25	26	27	28	29	30	

DECEMBER
M	TU	W	TH	F	SA	SU
						1
2	3	4	5	6	7	8
9	10	11	12	13	14	15
16	17	18	19	20	21	22
23	24	25	26	27	28	29
30	31					

Argentina	Jan 1, Feb 20–21, Mar 24, Apr 2, Apr 6–7, May 1, May 25, Jun 17, Jun 20, Jul 9, Aug 21, Oct 9, Nov 20, Dec 8, Dec 25
Australia	Jan 1–2, Jan 26, Mar 6 (WA), Mar 13 (TAS, VIC, ACT), Apr 7, Apr 8 (exc TAS, WA), Apr 9 (exc NT, WA), Apr 10, Apr 25, May 1 (NT, QLD), Jun 5 (WA), Jun 12 (exc QLD, WA), Aug 7 (NT), Sep 25 (WA), Oct 2 (ACT, NSW, QLD, SA), Dec 24 (exc NT, SA), Dec 25, Dec 26, Dec 31 (NT, SA)
Austria	Jan 1, Jan 6, Apr 10, May 1, May 18, May 29, Jun 8, Aug 15, Oct 26, Nov 1, Dec 8, Dec 25–26
Belgium	Jan 1, Apr 10, May 1, May 18, May 29, Jul 21, Aug 15, Nov 1, Nov 11, Dec 25
Brazil	Jan 1, Apr 21, May 1, Sep 7, Oct 12, Nov 2, Nov 15, Dec 25
Canada	Jan 1, Apr 7, Apr 10, May 22, Jul 1, Aug 7, Sep 4, Oct 2, Oct 9, Nov 11, Nov 13, Dec 25–26
China	Jan 1, Jan 21–27, Apr 3–5, May 1, Jun 22–23, Sep 29, Oct 1–7
Denmark	Jan 1, Apr 6–10, May 5, May 18, May 28–29, Dec 25–26
Finland	Jan 1, Jan 6, Apr 7–10, May 1, May 18, May 28, Jun 23–24, Nov 4, Dec 6, Dec 24–26
France	Jan 1, Apr 10, May 1, May 8, May 18, May 28–29, Jul 14, Aug 15, Nov 1, Nov 11, Dec 25
Germany	Jan 1, Apr 7, Apr 10, May 1, May 18, May 29, Oct 3, Dec 25–26
Greece	Jan 1, Jan 6, Feb 27, Mar 25, Apr 14, Apr 16–17, May 1, Jun 4–5, Aug 15, Oct 28, Dec 25–26
India	Jan 1, Jan 26, Feb 18, Mar 8, Mar 30, Apr 7, Apr 14, Apr 22, Jun 29, Jul 29, Aug 15, Sep 7, Sep 28, Oct 2, Oct 24, Nov 12, Nov 27, Dec 25
Indonesia	Jan 1, Jan 22, Feb 18, Mar 22, Apr 7, Apr 22–23, May 1, May 6, May 18, Jun 1, Jun 29, Jul 19, Aug 17, Sep 27, Dec 25
Israel	Apr 6, Apr 12, Apr 26, May 26, Sep 16–17, Sep 25, Sep 30, Oct 7
Italy	Jan 1, Jan 6, Apr 9–10, Apr 25, May 1, Jun 2, Aug 15, Nov 1, Dec 8, Dec 25–26
Japan	Jan 1–2, Jan 9, Feb 11, Feb 23, Mar 20, Apr 29, May 3–5, Jul 17, Aug 11, Sep 18, Sept 23, Oct 9, Nov 3, Nov 23

Luxembourg	Jan 1, Apr 10, May 1, May 9, May 18, May 29, Jun 23, Aug 15, Nov 1, Dec 25–26
Mexico	Jan 1, Feb 5–6, Mar 20, May 1, Sep 16, Nov 20, Dec 25
Netherlands	Jan 1, Apr 7, Apr 9–10, Apr 27, May 5, May 18, May 28–29, Dec 25–26
New Zealand	Jan 1–3, Feb 6, Apr 7, Apr 10, Apr 11, Apr 25, Jun 5, Oct 20, Dec 25–26
Nigeria	Jan 1–2, Apr 7, Apr 10, Apr 21–22, May 1, Jun 12, Jul 28–29, Sep 27, Oct 1–2, Dec 25–26
Pakistan	Feb 5, Mar 23, Apr 22–24, May 1, Jun 29–30, Jun 28–29, Aug 14, Sep 28, Dec 25
Poland	Jan 1, Jan 6, Apr 9–10, May 1, May 3, May 28, Jun 8, Aug 15, Nov 1, Nov 11, Dec 25–26
Portugal	Jan 1, Apr 7, Apr 9, Apr 25, May 1, Jun 8, Jun 10, Aug 15, Oct 5, Nov 1, Dec 1, Dec 8, Dec 25
Republic of Ireland	Jan 1, Mar 17, Apr 10, May 1, Jun 5, Aug 7, Oct 30, Dec 25–26
Russia	Jan 1–6, Jan 7, Jan 9, Feb 23, Mar 8, May 1, May 9, Jun 12, Nov 4, Nov 6
South Africa	Jan 1–2, Mar 21, Apr 7, Apr 10, Apr 27, May 1, Jun 16, Aug 9, Sep 24–25, Dec 16, Dec 25–26
Spain	Jan 2, Jan 6, Apr 7, May 1, Aug 15, Oct 12, Nov 1, Dec 6, Dec 8, Dec 25
Sweden	Jan 1, Jan 6, Apr 7, Apr 9–10, May 1, May 18, May 28, Jun 6, Jun 24, Nov 4, Dec 25–26
Turkey	Jan 1, Apr 21–23, May 1, May 19, Jun 28–Jul 1, Jul 15, Aug 30, Oct 29
United Kingdom	Jan 1–2, Mar 17 (NI), Apr 7, Apr 10 (exc SCO), May 1, May 29, Jul 12 (NI), Aug 7 (SCO), Aug 28 (exc SCO), Nov 30 (SCO), Dec 25–26
United States	Jan 1–2, Jan 16, May 29, Jul 4, Sep 4, Oct 9, Nov 11, Nov 23, Dec 25

WELCOME TO 2023!

So here we are! With a brand new year before us. A fresh chapter during which to seek new possibilities, create new memories and make "every day matter".

I sometimes find that this time of year can be tinged with a slight sense of nostalgia, yet it also brings a sense of hope and potential, which is where I choose to place my emphasis. So I hope this diary will help you to create a year that lives up to this hope, fulfils this potential and feels true to you.

As well as allowing space for you to organize your day-to-day life, the diary offers a new positive theme for you to focus on each month. And within each of these themes – Vision, Balance, Comfort, Gentleness, Release, Positivity, Trust, Fortitude, Rest, Evolving, Listening and Vulnerability – you will find a range of thought-provoking weekly quotes and prompts, as well as monthly review questions, all of which aim to inspire you to live openly and authentically throughout the year.

I hope 2023 is a year of self-discovery, fulfilment and, most of all, happiness for you and all of those you love.

JANUARY

VISION

We all have things that we'd like to do, ways that we'd like to be and goals that we'd like to reach, but our own needs and wants often accidentally get pushed to the bottom of our agendas. So what better way to start the year than with a refreshed vision of how we'd like our life to look during the twelve months ahead?

Although there will always be bumps along life's journey, we all deserve to be happy – living a life that we're content with. Looking inwards to review what has, and hasn't, been working for us of late can be a great starting point for this, allowing us to then pinpoint – and create a vision of – both the things that we'd like to maintain or enhance and the other things that we'd like to change for the better.

Use this month's weekly prompts to gradually build your vision of what would be ideal for you, so that you can then work out how to best put these things into action.

AFFIRMATION OF THE MONTH

My vision is important – it reflects my values, my hopes, my happiness and what is best for me

DEC 26 – JAN 1
vision

26 / MONDAY
Boxing Day
Kwanzaa begins

27 / TUESDAY

28 / WEDNESDAY

NOTES

> "Your vision will become clear only when you can look into your own heart."

CARL GUSTAV JUNG (1875–1961), SWISS PSYCHIATRIST

29 / THURSDAY

30 / FRIDAY ☽

31 / SATURDAY
New Year's Eve

1 / SUNDAY
New Year's Day
Kwanzaa ends

BUILD ON HOW YOU FEEL *NOW*

To know what we would like to see in our futures, it's important to understand how we feel in our lives *now*. This week, take time to look inwards and see what you like about yourself and your current life. Make a list and keep it as a reminder that these are things to embrace and do more of during the coming year.

JAN 2 - JAN 8

vision

2 / MONDAY
New Year's Day Public
Holiday

3 / TUESDAY
Public Holiday (SCO, NZ)

4 / WEDNESDAY

NOTES

> "Originality consists not in a new manner but in a new vision."

EDITH WHARTON (1862–1937), AMERICAN NOVELIST

5 / THURSDAY
Twelfth Night

6 / FRIDAY ○
Epiphany

7 / SATURDAY
Christmas Day (Orthodox)

8 / SUNDAY

ENVISAGE YOUR IDEAL FUTURE

What would your unique, ideal vision for the year ahead be? Would you like to spend more time with friends and family? Would you like to prioritize wellbeing? This week, have a think about how you could make some small changes to put your visions into action.

9 / MONDAY	10 / TUESDAY	11 / WEDNESDAY

NOTES

> "The only thing worse than being
> blind is having sight but no vision."

HELEN KELLER (1880–1968), AMERICAN DEAF-BLIND AUTHOR AND ACTIVIST

12 / THURSDAY

13 / FRIDAY

14 / SATURDAY
New Year's Day (Orthodox)

15 / SUNDAY ☾

CREATE A VISION BOARD

Vision boards can be a wonderful way to create
a visual representation of your hopes, dreams
and goals. Take time out this week to envisage
your ideal state of being. Then find images
and quotes that fit this vision and use them to
create a visually appealing board that can act as
a reminder of what is most important to you.

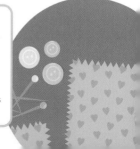

JAN 16 – JAN 22

vision

16 / MONDAY
Martin Luther King Jr Day

17 / TUESDAY

18 / WEDNESDAY

NOTES

> "Vision is the art of seeing what
> is invisible to others."

JONATHAN SWIFT (1667–1745), ANGLO-IRISH AUTHOR AND POET

19 / THURSDAY	20 / FRIDAY ≈	21 / SATURDAY ●

22 / SUNDAY
Chinese New Year (Year of
the Rabbit)

FOCUS ON PEOPLE AND PLACES

We all have those people and places in our life
that mean the world to us. The ones that fill us
up, making us feel loved, happy and whole. Take
a moment this week to identify who or what
these are for you. Then visualize how you can
incorporate more of them – and the joy and love
that they bring to you – into your life this year.

JAN 23 – JAN 29

vision

23 / MONDAY	24 / TUESDAY	25 / WEDNESDAY
		Burns Night (SCO)

NOTES

> "Just because a man lacks the use of
> his eyes doesn't mean he lacks vision."

STEVIE WONDER (1950–PRESENT), BLIND AMERICAN MUSICIAN

26 / THURSDAY
Australia Day

27 / FRIDAY
International Holocaust
Remembrance Day

28 / SATURDAY ☽

29 / SUNDAY

TACKLE YOUR FEARS

Sometimes your visions for the future can be
made difficult due to fears. For example, you
want more independence, but you're nervous
about driving on your own. This week, identify
something that's stopping you from reaching a
particular goal and try to envisage how you can
tackle the problem in order to move forward.

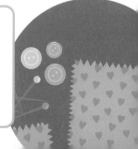

JANUARY OVERVIEW

M	TU	W	TH	F	SA	SU
26	27	28	29	30	31	1
2	3	4	5	6	7	8
9	10	11	12	13	14	15
16	17	18	19	20	21	22
23	24	25	26	27	28	29
30	31	1	2	3	4	5

This month I am grateful for . . .

_____

_____

_____

_____

_____

_____

REFLECTIONS ON VISION

How have you found focusing on your visions for the future this month?

What are the main things that you have realized when visualizing your own happiness for the coming year?

In what ways will you implement your positive visions in the future?

FEBRUARY

BALANCE

It's crucial to strive for some balance in our daily lives for the sake of our overall health and wellbeing. When we feel balanced, we tend to feel calmer and more grounded, we have increased focus, we function better in our relationships, we perform better at work and we generally have a better state of both physical and emotional wellbeing.

Yet balance tends to be a quality that people find hard to attain. As life is rarely straightforward, achieving an overall sense of balance is tough! Sometimes the scales tip more in one direction and at other times they tip the other way, but the important thing is that we recognize when such imbalances creep in and take the steps needed to find a sense of stability again.

This month, use the weekly prompts to help you identify in what areas of your life you could perhaps find more balance.

AFFIRMATION OF THE MONTH

I strive for balance in all aspects of my life – for my own health and wellbeing

JAN 30 – FEB 5

Balance

30 / MONDAY	31 / TUESDAY	1 / WEDNESDAY
		St Brigid's Day (Imbolc)
		Black History Month begins
		(CAN, USA)

NOTES

> "Balance is the perfect state of still water. Let that be our model. It remains quiet within and is not disturbed on the surface."

CONFUCIUS (c. 551–479 BCE), CHINESE PHILOSOPHER

2 / THURSDAY
Candlemas
Groundhog Day

3 / FRIDAY

4 / SATURDAY

5 / SUNDAY ○

IDENTIFY AREAS OF IMBALANCE

Life will always have its ups and downs and its stressful moments. This week, look at the current causes of imbalance and stress in your life. Ask yourself "What things would need to be removed from my life for me to feel more balanced and still? And could I change or say goodbye to at least some of these things?"

FEB 6 – FEB 12

Balance

6 / MONDAY
Waitangi Day

7 / TUESDAY

8 / WEDNESDAY

NOTES

> "Life is like riding a bicycle.
> To keep your balance, you must keep moving."

ALBERT EINSTEIN (1879–1955), GERMAN PHYSICIST

9 / THURSDAY

10 / FRIDAY

11 / SATURDAY

12 / SUNDAY
Abraham Lincoln's birthday

FIND YOUR MOST BALANCED SELF

This week, take time to think about when you
are your best self – at your most contented,
happy and balanced? Is this a strong feeling?
Do you feel it often? And what helps to bring
it on? Then consider how you might be able to
enhance and build on this ever-shifting sense
of balance moving forward.

FEB 13 – FEB 19

Balance

13 / MONDAY ☾

14 / TUESDAY
St Valentine's Day

15 / WEDNESDAY
Nirvana Day

NOTES

> "Moderate in order to taste
> the joys of life in abundance."

EPICURUS (c. 341–270 BCE), GREEK PHILOSOPHER

16 / THURSDAY	17 / FRIDAY	18 / SATURDAY

19 / SUNDAY ♓

DIGITAL BOUNDARIES

Balance can be difficult to achieve due to
the 24/7 pull of online life. This week, think
about boundaries you could put in place. You
could allocate time on certain apps, remove
notifications from your cellphone or keep work
emails to your computer only. See if this makes
a difference to your sense of balance.

FEB 20 – FEB 26

BaLance

20 / MONDAY ●
Presidents' Day

21 / TUESDAY
Shrove Tuesday
Losar (Tibetan New Year)

22 / WEDNESDAY
Ash Wednesday

NOTES

> "Life is a balance of holding on and letting go."

RUMI (1207–1273), PERSIAN POET

23 / THURSDAY

24 / FRIDAY

25 / SATURDAY

26 / SUNDAY

IT'S OKAY TO SAY NO

It can be hard to say no to people, but remember that it's not possible to do everything! So when someone asks you to do something you don't have time for or don't want to do, remind yourself that no (especially if said with kindness) is an okay answer. Sometimes we need to say no to others in order to regain some personal balance.

FEBRUARY OVERVIEW

M	TU	W	TH	F	SA	SU
30	31	1	2	3	4	5
6	7	8	9	10	11	12
13	14	15	16	17	18	19
20	21	22	23	24	25	26
27	28	1	2	3	4	5

This month I am grateful for . . .

REFLECTIONS ON BALANCE

How have you found thinking about balance in your life this month?

What are the main things that you have realized when looking at how balanced your current life feels?

In what ways will you implement change for a more balanced and calm future?

MARCH

COMFORT

We all need comfort in our lives, especially during stressful or difficult times. Comfort is a hug for the soul and a calm, safe harbour from any storms going on around us.

But comfort can mean many different things to different people, depending on our personal likes and needs. As such, we all tend to have our own little ways of self-soothing that we can turn to in times of need. This might be changing into your comfiest clothes after a long day at work; the hug of a loved one; the sound of their voice; listening to your favourite song; watching your favourite film; or the familiar smell of your morning coffee that brings with it a wave of ease. All very different, but all equally as important.

Getting to know and be able to tap into your own sources of true comfort in the pages ahead can be a real lifeline for helping you through tough days, as well as for boosting your overall happiness and wellbeing.

AFFIRMATION OF THE MONTH

I am worthy of comfort, love and support

FEB 27 – MAR 5

comfort

27 / MONDAY ☽

28 / TUESDAY

1 / WEDNESDAY
St David's Day

NOTES

> "Cure sometimes, treat often, comfort always."
>
> HIPPOCRATES (c. 460–370 BCE), GREEK PHYSICIAN

2 / THURSDAY
World Book Day

3 / FRIDAY

4 / SATURDAY

5 / SUNDAY

YOU DESERVE COMFORT

Everyone needs and deserves comfort. But it can
be difficult to know how to soothe ourselves in
times of stress. So this week, turn to the Inspired
Journalling section at the back of the diary and
create your very own Comfort List. That way, you
have a readymade list of things to turn to and use
as a helpful prompt any time you need it.

6 / MONDAY

Labour Day (WA)
Purim begins at sundown

7 / TUESDAY ○

8 / WEDNESDAY

International Women's Day
Holi (Festival of Colours)

NOTES

> "There is nothing like staying
> at home for real comfort."

JANE AUSTEN (1775–1817), ENGLISH NOVELIST

9 / THURSDAY

10 / FRIDAY

11 / SATURDAY

12 / SUNDAY
Daylight Saving Time starts
(CAN, USA)

COMFORT IN REPETITION

Often we find comfort in the things we know
well. They offer a soothing sense of stability and
predictability. So is there a film, TV show or book
that you always go back to, knowing it will offer
you this kind of reassurance? Take some time this
week to watch or read it and really soak up that
familiar feeling – like being with an old friend.

13 / MONDAY
Commonwealth Day
Public Holiday (ACT, SA,
TAS, VIC)

14 / TUESDAY

15 / WEDNESDAY ☾

NOTES

> "For even the wildest animals love comfort and warmth, and they survive the winter only because they are so careful to secure them."

HENRY DAVID THOREAU (1817–1962), AMERICAN POET AND PHILOSOPHER

16 / THURSDAY

17 / FRIDAY
St Patrick's Day

18 / SATURDAY

19 / SUNDAY
Mother's Day (UK)

VISIT YOUR HAPPY PLACE

A familiar environment that offers comfort and reassurance is a wonderful thing. It can give a space to just "be" – where we feel calm and at ease. So do you have such a "happy place"? If so, try to pay it a visit this week, or sometime soon. If not, see if you can discover one – whether at home or elsewhere.

MAR 20 – MAR 26

comfort

20 / MONDAY ♈
Spring Equinox (UK, ROI, CAN, USA)

21 / TUESDAY ●
Autumn Equinox (AUS, NZ)

22 / WEDNESDAY
Ramadan begins at sundown

NOTES

> "Kind words do not cost much.
> Yet they accomplish much."

BLAISE PASCAL (1623–1662), FRENCH MATHEMATICIAN

23 / THURSDAY

24 / FRIDAY

25 / SATURDAY

26 / SUNDAY
British Summer Time begins

WORDS OF COMFORT

Words can hold so much power. Take a moment
this week to write down some words of comfort
for yourself and stick them in a place that you will
see often, such as on the fridge door or bathroom
mirror. Whether a favourite song lyric, quote or
self-made affirmation, let the words be there for
you any time you need them.

MARCH OVERVIEW

M	TU	W	TH	F	SA	SU
27	28	1	2	3	4	5
6	7	8	9	10	11	12
13	14	15	16	17	18	19
20	21	22	23	24	25	26
27	28	29	30	31	1	2

This month I am grateful for . . .

_____

_____

_____

_____

_____

_____

REFLECTIONS ON COMFORT

How have you embraced more of a sense of comfort in your life this month?

How has trying to dedicate more time to self-comfort felt for you?

Would you like to continue trying to offer yourself more comfort and reassurance in the months ahead? If so, how?

APRIL

GENTLENESS

The art of gentleness is a wonderful thing. But, unfortunately, such "softness" can sometimes be seen in today's world as a weakness that might prevent you from "succeeding". However, the truth is that to be gentle in a world that is often not that gentle to live in shows much courage and strength.

When we open ourselves up to being gentle, it allows us to create deeper connections not only with each other but also with ourselves. It creates more kindness, compassion and warmth in the world, which helps us to heal, and therefore thrive. And it changes lives by making us feel more authentic and less alone.

There is so much need for gentleness in this world – and so much to gain from it. Gentleness really can be a powerful gift to the world.

AFFIRMATION OF THE MONTH

I will remember just how much strength there is in being gentle, even if I'm told otherwise

MAR 27 – APR 2

Gentleness

27 / MONDAY	28 / TUESDAY	29 / WEDNESDAY ☽

NOTES

> "Let gentleness my strong enforcement be."

WILLIAM SHAKESPEARE (1564–1616), ENGLISH PLAYWRIGHT

30 / THURSDAY

_____

_____

_____

_____

_____

_____

_____

_____

_____

31 / FRIDAY

_____

_____

_____

_____

_____

_____

_____

_____

_____

1 / SATURDAY
April Fools' Day

_____

_____

_____

2 / SUNDAY
Palm Sunday

_____

_____

_____

_____

WHAT IS GENTLENESS TO YOU?

The word gentleness can be used to describe
many things, both emotional and physical. Have
a think about what the word means to you and
in what ways you already practise it (or not). For
example, consider how you treat yourself, your
family, your friends and even strangers?

APR 3 – APR 9

Gentleness

3 / MONDAY

4 / TUESDAY

5 / WEDNESDAY
Passover begins at sundown

NOTES

> "In a gentle way, you can shake the world."

MAHATMA GANDHI (1869–1948), INDIAN LAWYER, ACTIVIST AND LEADER

6 / THURSDAY ○
Maundy Thursday

7 / FRIDAY
Good Friday

8 / SATURDAY
Easter Saturday

9 / SUNDAY
Easter Sunday

THE IMPACT OF GENTLENESS

Think about specific times when you have been
gentle with others. What did you do and how do
you think this impacted them? Had you acted
differently, would the outcome have differed?
And how can you show more gentleness to the
people in your life moving forward – through
your thoughts, words and actions?

APR 10 – APR 16

Gentleness

10 / MONDAY
Easter Monday

11 / TUESDAY

12 / WEDNESDAY

NOTES

> "Nothing is so strong as gentleness,
> nothing so gentle as real strength."

ST FRANCIS DE SALES (1567–1622), FRENCH BISHOP

13 / THURSDAY ☾
Passover ends at sundown

14 / FRIDAY

15 / SATURDAY

16 / SUNDAY
Easter (Orthodox)

BE KIND TO YOURSELF

If you aren't being gentle inwardly, toward
yourself, then you will never be able to be fully
gentle with others. This week, take time to
do a few kind, nourishing things for yourself.
Everyone needs to refill their reserves of
gentleness in order to stay strong!

APR 17 – APR 23

Gentleness

17 / MONDAY
Easter Monday (Orthodox)

_____
_____
_____
_____
_____
_____
_____
_____
_____
_____
_____
_____

18 / TUESDAY

_____
_____
_____
_____
_____
_____
_____
_____
_____
_____
_____
_____

19 / WEDNESDAY

_____
_____
_____
_____
_____
_____
_____
_____
_____
_____
_____
_____

NOTES

_____
_____
_____
_____

> "Gentleness is the ability to ... be free from bitterness and consciousness, having tranquillity and stability in the spirit."

ARISTOTLE (c. 384–322 BCE), GREEK PHILOSOPHER

20 / THURSDAY ♊
Ramadan ends at sundown

21 / FRIDAY
Eid al-Fitr

22 / SATURDAY
Earth Day

23 / SUNDAY
St George's Day

REFRAME YOUR PAST EXPERIENCES

Sometimes our past experiences affect how we act in the present. For example, if we have previously been shamed for showing our gentler side, it can be hard to show it again now. This week, try to break down any blocks to gentleness that you may have once built up.

APR 24 – APR 30

Gentleness

24 / MONDAY	25 / TUESDAY	26 / WEDNESDAY
	Anzac Day	

NOTES

> "One who knows how to show and
> to accept kindness will be a friend
> better than any possession."

SOPHOCLES (c. 496–406 BCE), GREEK PLAYWRIGHT

27 / THURSDAY ☽   28 / FRIDAY   29 / SATURDAY

30 / SUNDAY

APPRECIATE GENTLENESS
FROM OTHERS

When someone takes the time to show you
kindness, it can be a validating experience. Think
about a time when someone was gentle toward
you. How did it make you feel? Write a message
to that person to thank them, even if you don't
feel comfortable sending it to them.

APRIL OVERVIEW

M	TU	W	TH	F	SA	SU
27	28	29	30	31	1	2
3	4	5	6	7	8	9
10	11	12	13	14	15	16
17	18	19	20	21	22	23
24	25	26	27	28	29	30

This month I am grateful for . . .

_____

_____

_____

_____

_____

_____

_____

REFLECTIONS ON GENTLENESS

How has focusing on being more gentle this month affected you?

_____

_____

_____

_____

_____

_____

How did it feel to be more tuned in to receiving the gentleness of others?

_____

_____

_____

_____

_____

_____

In what ways do you think embracing your gentler side can help you in the future?

_____

_____

_____

_____

_____

_____

_____

MAY

RELEASE

There's nothing more freeing than being able to release things that are no longer serving us well, whether physical objects or thoughts and emotions that are weighing us down.

The process of letting go can, of course, be difficult, as some of the things may even have started to feel, over time, as if they're part of us (which they're not)! But once you're ready to let go, it can lead to a deep sense of peace and wellbeing, as the alternative – of carrying all your old, heavy baggage around with you throughout each and every busy day – would be just so exhausting!

Learning to acknowledge that not everything that you've been carrying was actually even your weight to bear in the first place is crucial, as this will allow you to release things and move on. So use the weekly prompts this month to help you do just that.

AFFIRMATION OF THE MONTH

I release with grace all that no longer serves me

MAY 1 – MAY 7

1 / MONDAY
Early May Bank Holiday
(UK, ROI)
Beltane
May Day

_____

_____

_____

_____

_____

_____

_____

_____

_____

_____

_____

2 / TUESDAY

_____

_____

_____

_____

_____

_____

_____

_____

_____

_____

_____

_____

3 / WEDNESDAY

_____

_____

_____

_____

_____

_____

_____

_____

_____

_____

_____

_____

NOTES

_____

_____

_____

> "When I let go of what I am,
> I become what I might be."

LAO TZU (6TH CENTURY BCE), CHINESE PHILOSOPHER

4 / THURSDAY	5 / FRIDAY ○	6 / SATURDAY
	Cinco de Mayo	
	Vesak Day (Buddha Day)	

7 / SUNDAY

TALKING IS A TONIC

We often ruminate over things that are
bothering us, torturing ourselves by reliving
details in our head. This week, try telling
someone about something that's weighing on
your mind. Getting it out in the open can feel
like an enormous weight lifted.

MAY 8 – MAY 14

release

8 / MONDAY	9 / TUESDAY	10 / WEDNESDAY

NOTES

> "There is never any need to get worked up ... about things you can't control. These things are not asking to be judged by you. Leave them alone."

MARCUS AURELIUS (121–180 CE), ROMAN EMPEROR

11 / THURSDAY

12 / FRIDAY ☾

13 / SATURDAY

14 / SUNDAY
Mother's Day (CAN, USA, AUS, NZ)

FOCUS ON WHAT YOU CAN CONTROL

The feeling of not being in control can cause us to hold on to a lot of tension. This week, think about how you could regain some control in a certain situation, such as by taking a different path. If you find yourself struggling with this, try repeating "I concentrate on what I can control and I release everything that I can't."

MAY 15 – MAY 21

release

15 / MONDAY	16 / TUESDAY	17 / WEDNESDAY

NOTES

> "We must be willing to let go of the life we've planned, so as to have the life that is waiting for us."

JOSEPH CAMPBELL (1904-1987), AMERICAN PROFESSOR AND AUTHOR

18 / THURSDAY
Ascension Day

19 / FRIDAY ●

20 / SATURDAY

21 / SUNDAY ♊

WRITE IT DOWN

It's often hard to release negative emotions as they can feel so tied up with our dashed hopes and dreams. But the act of writing can be a great way of getting such burdens out of your head – and allowing you to move on! This week, identify something you're holding on to and write it all down. Then how do you feel?

MAY 22 – MAY 28

22 / MONDAY
Victoria Day (CAN, except NS, NU, QC)

23 / TUESDAY

24 / WEDNESDAY

NOTES

> "Some of us think holding on makes us strong,
> but sometimes it is letting go."

HERMAN HESSE (1877–1962), GERMAN-BORN SWISS AUTHOR

25 / THURSDAY	26 / FRIDAY	27 / SATURDAY ☽
		28 / SUNDAY
		Pentecost (Whit Sunday)

IS IT ALL REALLY NECESSARY?

In today's digital age, we're often expected to
be available 24/7. This week, consider whether
you could let go of some of the demands you
place on yourself. Maybe you could take work
emails off your cellphone? See how setting new
boundaries like this makes you feel.

MAY OVERVIEW

M	TU	W	TH	F	SA	SU
1	2	3	4	5	6	7
8	9	10	11	12	13	14
15	16	17	18	19	20	21
22	23	24	25	26	27	28
29	30	31	1	2	3	4

This month I am grateful for . . .

_____

_____

_____

_____

_____

_____

_____

_____

REFLECTIONS ON RELEASE

How have you found focusing on releasing difficult thoughts and feelings this month?

_____

_____

_____

_____

_____

_____

How has putting more emphasis on what you can control felt, rather than worrying about what you can't control?

_____

_____

_____

_____

_____

In what ways do you think letting go of more things that weigh you down could help you in the future?

_____

_____

_____

_____

_____

JUne

POSITIVITY

What does the word positivity mean to you? For some people these days, it can have fairly negative connotations due to the idea of it requiring "good vibes only" and therefore not allowing any negative stuff in. But this doesn't have to be its meaning.

Personally, I see positivity as a gentle optimism. A small beacon of light in the darkness. A metaphorical hand on the shoulder when things are feeling tough. As such, I don't see it as being about shutting out the negative things, the difficult bits or the dark days. Instead, I see it as knowing that, although these dark times exist, there's hope for a better and brighter time soon. A belief that, although things may feel overwhelming right now, you have the capability and the resilience to make it through.

Use the weekly prompts to help you connect with a sense of positivity that feels useful to you – so that you can hopefully then start to implement it in your daily life.

AFFIRMATION OF THE MONTH

Even in the darkness,
I trust, with positivity,
that the light will find
me again

MAY 29 – JUN 4

positivity

29 / MONDAY
Spring Bank Holiday (UK)
Memorial Day (USA)

30 / TUESDAY

31 / WEDNESDAY

NOTES

> ## "Keep your face to the sunshine and you cannot see a shadow."

HELEN KELLER (1880–1968), AMERICAN DEAF-BLIND AUTHOR AND ACTIVIST

1 / THURSDAY	2 / FRIDAY	3 / SATURDAY
		4 / SUNDAY ○

LOOK FOR THE POSITIVE

Sometimes the toughest periods in our lives can help us to reach important realizations that impact how we move forward. Think of a particularly hard time for you and, rather than letting it drag you down, consider what you learnt from the experience.

JUN 5 – JUN 11

positivity

5 / MONDAY
June Bank Holiday (ROI)
Queen's birthday celebrated
(NZ)
Western Australia Day (WA)

6 / TUESDAY

7 / WEDNESDAY

NOTES

> ## "Positive anything is better than negative nothing."
> ELBERT HUBBARD (1856–1915), AMERICAN WRITER

8 / THURSDAY

9 / FRIDAY

10 / SATURDAY ☾

_____

_____

_____

_____

_____

_____

11 / SUNDAY

_____

_____

_____

_____

_____

WHAT ARE YOU LOOKING FORWARD TO?

It's always good to have something positive to look forward to. This week, consider if you have anything exciting planned that could help you through the more mundane days. If not, make a plan, whether a meeting with a friend or getting away for a few days. Then see how you feel.

JUN 12 – JUN 18

positivity

12 / MONDAY
Queen's birthday celebrated
(AUS, except QLD, WA)

_____

_____

_____

_____

_____

_____

_____

_____

_____

_____

_____

_____

13 / TUESDAY

_____

_____

_____

_____

_____

_____

_____

_____

_____

_____

_____

_____

14 / WEDNESDAY

_____

_____

_____

_____

_____

_____

_____

_____

_____

_____

_____

_____

NOTES

> "For every minute you are angry,
> you lose sixty seconds of happiness."

RALPH WALDO EMERSON (1803–1882), AMERICAN PHILOSOPHER AND POET

15 / THURSDAY   16 / FRIDAY   17 / SATURDAY

18 / SUNDAY ●
Father's Day (UK, ROI,
CAN, USA)

POSITIVE SELF-TALK

The words we use when thinking and talking
about ourselves can often be akin to those of a
bully! This week, be aware of whether you are
kind and positive about yourself. Every time you
find yourself being mean or negative, gently stop
yourself. If you wouldn't say it to a friend, you
shouldn't be saying it to yourself.

JUN 19 – JUN 25

positivity

19 / MONDAY	20 / TUESDAY	21 / WEDNESDAY ♋
		Summer Solstice (UK, ROI, CAN, USA)

NOTES

> ## "The best way to cheer yourself up is to cheer someone else up."
>
> MARK TWAIN (1835–1910), AMERICAN AUTHOR

22 / THURSDAY
Winter Solstice (AUS, NZ)

23 / FRIDAY

24 / SATURDAY

25 / SUNDAY

SPREAD A LITTLE POSITIVITY

A small act of kindness or positivity can change someone's whole day. This week, do something nice for someone, whether buying a stranger a coffee or leaving a kind anonymous note on a public bench. It might seem insignificant to you, but to someone else it could be the positive lifeline that they have needed.

JUNE OVERVIEW

M	TU	W	TH	F	SA	SU
29	30	31	1	2	3	4
5	6	7	8	9	10	11
12	13	14	15	16	17	18
19	20	21	22	23	24	25
26	27	28	29	30	1	2

This month I am grateful for . . .

_____

_____

_____

_____

_____

_____

REFLECTIONS ON POSITIVITY

How have you embraced more positivity in your life this month?

_____

_____

_____

_____

_____

_____

How has trying to give more time to being positive felt for you?

_____

_____

_____

_____

_____

Do you feel that positivity is something that comes naturally to you?
If not, is it something that you'd like to practise and implement more?

_____

_____

_____

_____

_____

JULY

TRUST

Trust can sometimes be a difficult thing to open ourselves up to, especially if we've had our trust betrayed in the past. Whether it's trusting others, the universe or ourselves, our past experiences can really affect our ability to lean into it again.

However, by closing ourselves off to trust, the likelihood is that we will miss out on all kinds of potentially wonderful experiences. So what kind of power and possibilities could we unlock if we focused on slowly rebuilding our trust in at least ourselves to start with? What new doors might we open if we could only start to trust in our own knowledge of what we want from life, what's best for us, our ability to navigate good versus bad and all the rest?

This month, use the weekly prompts to help you find and practise more trust in your day-to-day life – and therefore function from a place of increased authenticity and ease.

AFFIRMATION OF THE MONTH

I trust that I have
the ability to navigate
anything that life
throws at me

JUN 26 – JUL 2

Trust

26 / MONDAY ☽

27 / TUESDAY

28 / WEDNESDAY
Eid al-Adha (Feast of the Sacrifice) begins at sundown

NOTES

> "To persevere, trusting in what
> hopes he has, is courage in a man."

EURIPIDES (c. 480–406 BCE), GREEK POET

29 / THURSDAY

30 / FRIDAY

1 / SATURDAY
Canada Day

2 / SUNDAY

LET GO OF PAST HURTS

Have you ever had your trust taken for granted
or abused? Do you think this affected your
ability to trust? Without putting any pressure
on yourself, think about how you could start
to let go of betrayals of trust that you have
experienced in the past – in the knowledge
that it's for the best moving forward.

JUL 3 – JUL 9

Trust

3 / MONDAY ○

4 / TUESDAY
Independence Day (USA)

5 / WEDNESDAY

NOTES

> "The best way to find out if you can trust someone is to trust them."

ERNEST HEMINGWAY (1899–1961), AMERICAN AUTHOR

6 / THURSDAY   7 / FRIDAY   8 / SATURDAY

9 / SUNDAY

FOCUS ON THE GOOD

When was the last time you fully put your trust in someone and felt that it brought you something positive and worthwhile? Take time this week to write a list of these experiences that you can keep somewhere safe to remind yourself that allowing yourself to trust can be a wonderful thing.

JUL 10 – JUL 16

Trust

10 / MONDAY ☾

11 / TUESDAY

12 / WEDNESDAY
Orangemen's Day (NIR)

NOTES

> "Trust thyself: every heart vibrates to that iron string."

RALPH WALDO EMERSON (1803–1882), AMERICAN WRITER

13 / THURSDAY

14 / FRIDAY
Bastille Day

15 / SATURDAY

16 / SUNDAY

BUILD A VISION OF TRUST

Our own overthinking can often cloud our ability
to trust ourselves. Pinpoint something that's
worrying you this week and ask yourself, "If I
were to just trust myself, how would it look and
feel?" If this visualization helps you to feel more
at ease, try to tap into the feeling any time your
thoughts start to get the better of you.

JUL 17 – JUL 23

Trust

17 / MONDAY ●

18 / TUESDAY
Islamic New Year (first
day of Muharram) begins
at sundown

19 / WEDNESDAY

NOTES

> ## "As soon as you trust yourself, you will know how to live."

JOHANN WOLFGANG VON GOETHE (1749–1832), GERMAN WRITER

20 / THURSDAY   21 / FRIDAY   22 / SATURDAY ♌

23 / SUNDAY

A SELF-TRUST PEP TALK

Some days we wake up trusting ourselves, while others it is an uphill battle. This week, turn to the Inspired Journalling section at the back of the diary and write yourself a pep talk. Remind yourself why you should ignore the self-doubts. You can look back on this any time you need a boost of self-esteem.

JUL 24 – JUL 30

Trust

24 / MONDAY	25 / TUESDAY ☽	26 / WEDNESDAY

NOTES

> "Trust in dreams, for in them is hidden the gate to eternity."

KHALIL GIBRAN (1883–1931), LEBANESE WRITER

27 / THURSDAY

28 / FRIDAY

29 / SATURDAY

30 / SUNDAY

DON'T HOLD BACK

Have you ever felt like you've held back from
pursuing a goal due to lack of trust in yourself?
This week, make a step toward doing something
that you've always avoided for this reason. Even
the smallest step could open up a world
of possibilities.

JULY OVERVIEW

M	TU	W	TH	F	SA	SU
26	27	28	29	30	1	2
3	4	5	6	7	8	9
10	11	12	13	14	15	16
17	18	19	20	21	22	23
24	25	26	27	28	29	30
31	1	2	3	4	5	6

This month I am grateful for . . .

REFLECTIONS ON TRUST

In what ways have you explored your feelings toward trust this month?

_____

_____

_____

_____

_____

How does it feel to place your focus on trust and practise being more open to it in your life?

_____

_____

_____

_____

Do you think having more trust in yourself and your capabilities could lead to different outcomes in the future?

_____

_____

_____

_____

_____

AUGUST

FORTITUDE

Fortitude, bravery, courage – whatever we call this capacity to show strength in the face of adversity – we all have it within us. At times it might feel distant, but it is always there if we're willing to dig deep.

Life often pushes us to our limits of discomfort and pain. But it's often only once we're confronted with such testing times that we discover our true inner fortitude – the depths of which we were perhaps previously unaware.

As with many things in life, perceptions of fortitude are all relative – so what might be considered an act of great bravery by one person could be viewed as not such a big deal by another. It's therefore important to always acknowledge for ourselves when we have persevered and reached beyond what we thought possible.

Use this month's prompts to help you recognize and be proud of just how far your fortitude has brought you in life already, and just how much further it can carry you if you let it.

AFFIRMATION OF THE MONTH

I am stronger than I give myself credit for

JUL 31 – AUG 6

FORTITUDE

31 / MONDAY	1 / TUESDAY ○	2 / WEDNESDAY
	Lughnasadh (Lammas)	

NOTES

> "You're braver than you believe, stronger than you seem and smarter than you think."

A. A. MILNE (1882–1956), ENGLISH AUTHOR

3 / THURSDAY   4 / FRIDAY   5 / SATURDAY

_____   _____   _____

_____   _____   _____

_____   _____   _____

_____   _____   _____

_____   _____   _____

_____   _____   6 / SUNDAY

_____   _____   _____

_____   _____   _____

_____   _____   _____

_____   _____   _____

                                        _____

RECOGNIZE HOW STRONG YOU ARE

We often "keep on keeping on" in life, without
looking back at just how strong we've been. This
week, turn to the Inspired Journalling section
at the back of the diary and write a list of times
when fortitude has got you through something.
You can then turn to this list any time you need
a reminder of just how resilient you are!

AUG 7 – AUG 13

7 / MONDAY
August Bank Holiday (ROI, SCO)
Public Holiday (NSW, NT)

8 / TUESDAY ☾

9 / WEDNESDAY

NOTES

> "The longer I live, the more I think of the quality
> of fortitude ... men who fall, pick themselves
> up and stumble on ..."

THEODORE ROOSEVELT (1858–1919), 26th AMERICAN PRESIDENT

10 / THURSDAY 11 / FRIDAY 12 / SATURDAY

----

13 / SUNDAY

THERE'S STRENGTH IN ASKING FOR HELP

We often think that in order to be truly strong,
we need to face everything alone. This couldn't
be further from the truth! Reaching out for help
is often the bravest course of action. This week,
think about who your go-to people are when
you need support.

AUG 14 – AUG 20

FORTITUDE

14 / MONDAY	15 / TUESDAY	16 / WEDNESDAY ●

NOTES

> ## "It's not life that counts but the fortitude you bring into it."

JOHN GALSWORTHY (1867–1933), ENGLISH NOVELIST AND PLAYWRIGHT

17 / THURSDAY   18 / FRIDAY   19 / SATURDAY

20 / SUNDAY

SAY IT UNTIL YOU BELIEVE IT

Are there things that you find yourself struggling with on a regular basis? This week, complete the following sentence on a piece of paper and keep it somewhere safe for times when you need reminding of how strong you are: "I often struggle with ... and I show fortitude by ...".

AUG 21 – AUG 27

21 / MONDAY	22 / TUESDAY ♍	23 / WEDNESDAY

NOTES

> "Fortitude is the guard and
> support of the other virtues."

JOHN LOCKE (1632-1704), ENGLISH PHILOSOPHER

24 / THURSDAY ☽   25 / FRIDAY   26 / SATURDAY

----------------------------   ----------------------------

----------------------------   ----------------------------

----------------------------   ----------------------------

----------------------------   ----------------------------

----------------------------   ----------------------------   27 / SUNDAY

----------------------------   ----------------------------

----------------------------   ----------------------------

----------------------------   ----------------------------

----------------------------   ----------------------------

A SURGE IN FORTITUDE

Sometimes we don't feel brave enough to aim
for the goals we want. This week, ask yourself
this: "If I was given a mega-dose of fortitude
today, what action would I take toward a goal
that I've been unable to face?" Then see if
you can take that action today – and let the
momentum of fortitude take you from there!

AUGUST OVERVIEW

M	TU	W	TH	F	SA	SU
31	1	2	3	4	5	6
7	8	9	10	11	12	13
14	15	16	17	18	19	20
21	22	23	24	25	26	27
28	29	30	31	1	2	3

This month I am grateful for . . .

_____

_____

_____

_____

_____

_____

_____

REFLECTIONS ON FORTITUDE

In what ways have you acknowledged your own strength
in the face of adversity this month?

How did it feel to think about fortitude and what that looks like for you?

Do you think being able to recognize your moments of fortitude so far in life will help
you have more confidence in your fortitude for the future?

SEPTEMBER

REST

Rest and relaxation are just as essential to our health as movement and exercise. Yet they all too often get knocked to the bottom of our priority lists. And this means we end up needing rest and relaxation purely for recovery purposes, rather than embracing them for their own sake.

Many of us are unwilling to set down any of the many plates that we're spinning – in the belief that slowing down might be seen as "slacking" and that a certain amount of hard work has to be completed before we are "worthy" of any rest. But how can we be our best selves if our batteries never get recharged? And how can we be well and happy if we're not taking the time out that our bodies and minds so desperately need?

This month, try to find the time to integrate a healthier, more balanced amount of rest and relaxation into your life – because you deserve it!

AFFIRMATION OF THE MONTH

I am worthy of rest at any time, and I deserve to give my body and mind the time they need to recharge

AUG 28 – SEP 3

28 / MONDAY
Summer Bank Holiday (UK,
except SCO)

29 / TUESDAY

30 / WEDNESDAY

NOTES

> ## "Retire to the centre of your being, which is calmness."

PARAMAHANSA YOGANANDA (1893–1952), INDIAN MONK AND YOGI

31 / THURSDAY ○

1 / FRIDAY

2 / SATURDAY

3 / SUNDAY
Father's Day (AUS, NZ)

CHECK IN WITH YOURSELF

We often carry stress in our bodies without realizing it. This week, take a moment now and then to scan your body for areas of tension. Start at your face, noticing if you are clenching any muscles. Take a few deep breaths to release any tightness. Then continue like this down your body until you start to feel more relaxed.

SEP 4 – SEP 10

REST

4 / MONDAY
Labor Day (CAN, USA)

5 / TUESDAY

6 / WEDNESDAY ☾

NOTES

"Rest is the sweet sauce of labour."

PLUTARCH (c. 46 – 120 CE), GREEK HISTORIAN

7 / THURSDAY   8 / FRIDAY   9 / SATURDAY

10 / SUNDAY

MAKE TIME FOR YOURSELF

It's all too easy to neglect rest amid hectic
modern life. This week, identify an item on
your to-do list that can wait, and use the time
to instead do something restful. Gradually aim
to integrate more pockets of relaxation into
your days when you can.

SEP 11 – SEP 17

REST

11 / MONDAY	12 / TUESDAY	13 / WEDNESDAY

NOTES

> ## "Doing nothing is sometimes one of the highest of the duties of man."

G. K. CHESTERTON (1874–1936), ENGLISH WRITER

14 / THURSDAY	15 / FRIDAY ●	16 / SATURDAY
	Rosh Hashanah (Jewish New Year) begins at sundown	

17 / SUNDAY

MAKE A RELAXATION LIST

Things sometimes get so busy that it can feel as if we don't even remember how to switch off and relax! This week, turn to the Inspired Journalling section at the back of the diary and make a list of things that you know help you to unwind. You can then refer to this for tips on what to do any time you're feeling frazzled.

SEP 18 – SEP 24

REST

18 / MONDAY	19 / TUESDAY	20 / WEDNESDAY

NOTES

> "[The art of rest and relaxing] allows us to clear our minds, focus, and find creative solutions to problems."

THICH NHAT HANH (1926–PRESENT), BUDDHIST MONK

21 / THURSDAY
International Day of Peace

22 / FRIDAY ☽ ♎

23 / SATURDAY
Autumn Equinox (UK, ROI, CAN, USA)
Spring Equinox (AUS, NZ)

24 / SUNDAY
Yom Kippur (Day of Atonement) begins at sundown

LAUGHTER AS A TONIC

When was the last time you had a good laugh? Laughter can decrease heart rate and blood pressure, stimulate circulation and aid muscle relaxation – therefore reducing stress. This week, indulge yourself in something that makes you howl, whether a funny film, a TV programme or the company of a funny friend.

SEPTEMBER OVERVIEW

M	TU	W	TH	F	SA	SU
28	29	30	31	1	2	3
4	5	6	7	8	9	10
11	12	13	14	15	16	17
18	19	20	21	22	23	24
25	26	27	28	29	30	1

This month I am grateful for . . .

_____

_____

_____

_____

_____

_____

_____

REFLECTIONS ON REST

How have you implemented more rest and relaxation into your life this month?

Has paying more attention to rest and relaxation affected the way you feel emotionally and/or physically?

How will you continue to give yourself more rest and relaxation in the future?

OCTOBER

EVOLVING

Whether we realize it or not, we are always evolving. Every experience we go through shapes us and helps us to evolve into both the person that we are in the now and the person that we will become in the future.

Sometimes the change is gradual, which means it can be hard to see as it unfolds. Sometimes it's triggered by something bigger, which we can more obviously pinpoint. Whether the changes involve moments of joy and happiness or of difficulty and challenge, they all play their part in moulding us into the people we are as we move along life's journey.

Sometimes we may find ourselves settling into comfort zones that narrow the opportunity to experience the new things that keep us evolving – so it's important to remain aware of this and keep expanding our horizons.

This month's weekly prompts will help you to stay open to the beauty of evolving – embracing all that you meet along the way.

AFFIRMATION OF THE MONTH

I am always evolving, and my future is filled with endless possibilities

25 / MONDAY
Public Holiday (WA)

26 / TUESDAY
Milad un-Nabi (Birthday of
the Prophet Muhammed)
begins at sundown

27 / WEDNESDAY

NOTES

> "Endless forms most beautiful and wonderful
> have been, and are being, evolved."

CHARLES DARWIN (1809–1882), NATURALIST AND BIOLOGIST

28 / THURSDAY

29 / FRIDAY ○
Sukkot (Feast of the
Tabernacles) begins
at sundown

30 / SATURDAY

1 / SUNDAY
Black History Month begins
(UK)

YOUR EVOLUTION SO FAR

How often do you stop and actively look back on
how much you've evolved? This week, make a list
of pivotal moments in your life. You might have
graduated, got through a break-up, moved cities
– all of which have enabled great growth. Do
you give yourself the credit you deserve? Take a
moment to feel proud and really soak it all in.

OCT 2 – OCT 8
EVOLVING

2 / MONDAY
Public Holiday (ACT, NSW, QLD, SA)

3 / TUESDAY

4 / WEDNESDAY

NOTES

> "Evolve into the complete person
> you were intended to be."

OPRAH WINFREY (1954–PRESENT), AMERICAN TALK SHOW HOST

5 / THURSDAY   6 / FRIDAY ☾   7 / SATURDAY

_____   _____   _____
_____   _____   _____
_____   _____   _____
_____   _____   _____
_____   _____
_____   _____   8 / SUNDAY
_____   _____   _____
_____   _____   _____
_____   _____   _____
_____   _____   _____
_____   _____   _____

NEW PLACES, NEW EXPERIENCES

A great way to keep evolving is to keep seeking
out different experiences. This week, turn to the
Inspired Journalling section at the back of the
diary and write a list of all the new places you'd
like to visit. Anywhere at all! Use this list as
inspiration when you have some time off and
are wanting to take a little trip away.

OCT 9 – OCT 15

EVOLVING

9 / MONDAY
Thanksgiving (CAN)
Indigenous Peoples' Day/
Columbus Day

10 / TUESDAY

11 / WEDNESDAY

NOTES

> "We are always in transition. If you can just relax with that, you'll have no problem."

CHÖGYAM TRUNGPA (1939–1987), BUDDHIST MEDITATION MASTER

12 / THURSDAY

13 / FRIDAY

14 / SATURDAY ●

15 / SUNDAY

TINY STEPS ARE STILL STEPS

When we fall into comfortable routines, stepping outside of them can feel scary. It's okay to take things slowly – step by step. This might mean simply embracing a new genre of book this week or visiting a new restaurant for dinner. Give it a go, see how the change makes you feel and watch yourself grow from there ...

OCT 16 – OCT 22
EVOlVing

16 / MONDAY	17 / TUESDAY	18 / WEDNESDAY

NOTES

> "We cannot solve our problems with the same thinking we used when we created them."

ALBERT EINSTEIN (1879–1955), GERMAN PHYSICIST

19 / THURSDAY   20 / FRIDAY   21 / SATURDAY

22 / SUNDAY ☽

CHANGE YOUR MINDSET

Sometimes we know that it's time for a change in life as things no longer quite feel right. But this can be hard to admit and even harder to put into action, as it's tough to leave our comfort zones. This week, aim to identify a way of *thinking* about a particular area of your life that you could change to help yourself thrive more.

OCT 23 – OCT 29

EVOLVING

23 / MONDAY ♏
Labour Day (NZ)

24 / TUESDAY

25 / WEDNESDAY

NOTES

"The sun himself is weak when he first rises, and gathers strength and courage as the day goes on."

CHARLES DICKENS (1812–1870), ENGLISH NOVELIST

26 / THURSDAY   27 / FRIDAY   28 / SATURDAY ○

29 / SUNDAY
British Summer Time ends

GROWING THROUGH EXPERIENCE

This week, pinpoint an experience that you found particularly challenging in the past year. List what you learnt from it and how it's helped you to evolve as a person. Keep this list as a reminder that as hard as things may seem, you are more than capable of navigating your way through the hurdles life throws at you.

OCTOBER OVERVIEW

M	TU	W	TH	F	SA	SU
25	26	27	28	29	30	1
2	3	4	5	6	7	8
9	10	11	12	13	14	15
16	17	18	19	20	21	22
23	24	25	26	27	28	29
30	31	1	2	3	4	5

This month I am grateful for . . .

_____

_____

_____

_____

_____

_____

REFLECTIONS ON EVOLVING

How has it felt this month reflecting on how you've evolved through your life?

_____

_____

_____

_____

_____

Do you think you have evolved emotionally in the last month? If so, how?

_____

_____

_____

_____

_____

In what ways will you seek out more opportunities for learning and evolving in the future?

_____

_____

_____

_____

Don't miss out on next year's diary! See the back page for details on how to order your copy

NOVEMBER

LISTENING

The ability to really listen to others – and the experience of feeling heard by others – helps us to connect with them on a deeper level. It allows us not only to hear what one another are saying but also to understand where we are all coming from and what our experiences have been. Good listening skills also makes conversations feel more genuine, and therefore more enjoyable. However, listening is not something that always comes naturally, as many of us tend to be more concerned with what we are trying to say than what others are trying to say to us!

Nonetheless, listening is a skill that we can practise in order to get better at it! And while learning to listen to others is important, learning to listen to ourselves and our instincts is equally so.

Use the weekly prompts this month to help you practise listening more to both yourself and others in day-to-day life – becoming more in tune with everything around you as you do so.

AFFIRMATION OF THE MONTH

I listen to myself and honour my needs; I listen to others and honour their needs

OCT 30 – NOV 5
Listening

30 / MONDAY
October Bank Holiday
(ROI)

31 / TUESDAY
Halloween
Samhain

1 / WEDNESDAY
All Saints' Day

NOTES

> "Deep listening is the kind of listening that can help relieve the suffering of another person."

THICH NHAT HANH (1926–PRESENT), BUDDHIST MONK

2 / THURSDAY
All Souls' Day

3 / FRIDAY

4 / SATURDAY

5 / SUNDAY ☾
Guy Fawkes Day
Daylight Saving Time ends
(CAN, USA)

THE POWER OF FEELING HEARD

Sometimes we can feel like we're talking and
talking but not being fully listened to – and
this can make us feel frustrated and alone. This
week, turn to the Inspired Journalling section at
the back of the diary and make a list of times in
your life that you felt truly heard.

NOV 6 – NOV 12

Listening

6 / MONDAY

7 / TUESDAY

8 / WEDNESDAY

NOTES

> "I have learned a great deal from listening carefully. Most people never listen."

ERNEST HEMINGWAY (1899-1961), AMERICAN AUTHOR

9 / THURSDAY

10 / FRIDAY

11 / SATURDAY
Veterans Day (USA)
Remembrance Day (CAN)

12 / SUNDAY
Diwali
Remembrance Sunday (UK)

LISTEN TO YOUR OWN NEEDS

How often do you check in with your inner self
in terms of what you need and want out of life?
Take time this week to turn your attention inward
and connect with how you are feeling. Stressed?
Calm? Happy? What do you need more, or less,
of? And how could you achieve this? Know that
you deserve to put yourself first sometimes.

NOV 13 – NOV 19

Listening

13 / MONDAY ●	14 / TUESDAY	15 / WEDNESDAY

NOTES

> "The earth has music for those who listen."

WILLIAM SHAKESPEARE (1564–1616), ENGLISH PLAYWRIGHT

16 / THURSDAY　17 / FRIDAY　18 / SATURDAY

---

19 / SUNDAY

NATURE'S SOUNDTRACK

Tuning into the sounds of nature can be a
wonderful way of connecting with both the wider
world and ourselves. This week, try to get out and
listen in to the sounds of the wind between the
trees, the crunch of the ground beneath your
feet and the beautiful birdsong. Embrace all that
usually gets drowned out by our busy lives.

NOV 20 – NOV 26

20 / MONDAY ☽	21 / TUESDAY	22 / WEDNESDAY ↗
	World Hello Day	

NOTES

> "Wisdom is the reward you get for a lifetime of listening when you would rather have talked."

MARK TWAIN (1835–1910), AMERICAN AUTHOR

23 / THURSDAY
Thanksgiving (USA)

24 / FRIDAY

25 / SATURDAY

26 / SUNDAY

LISTEN MORE CAREFULLY

Do you consider yourself a good listener? If yes, what do you think makes you good? If not, how might you improve? For example, perhaps you need to worry less about what to say next. Or perhaps you should give the speaker more space before you respond. This week, pay attention to listening more intently.

NOVEMBER OVERVIEW

M	TU	W	TH	F	SA	SU
30	31	1	2	3	4	5
6	7	8	9	10	11	12
13	14	15	16	17	18	19
20	21	22	23	24	25	26
27	28	29	30	1	2	3

This month I am grateful for . . .

_____
_____
_____
_____
_____
_____

REFLECTIONS ON LISTENING

How have you found focusing on listening more this month?

_____

_____

_____

_____

_____

How has putting more emphasis on listening to yourself and your body felt?

_____

_____

_____

_____

In what ways do you think practising listening both to yourself and others could help you in the future?

_____

_____

_____

_____

DECEMBER

VULNERABILITY

Opening ourselves up to be more emotionally vulnerable can feel incredibly difficult, uncomfortable and exposing – so much so that we may feel the safer option is to protect ourselves by not showing vulnerability at all. However, the flip side is that sharing our authentic selves with others brings many benefits.

Being honest and vulnerable with ourselves leads to a deeper understanding of who we are and why we behave the way we do. Being honest and vulnerable with others leads to stronger, more trusting relationships, as it allows things to go beyond just surface-level conversation. Sharing our vulnerabilities with others helps them to see that they are not alone in their vulnerabilities, creating a deep sense of authentic connection.

Use the weekly prompts this month to see if you can get more in touch with your vulnerable side – and the strengths that lie within this.

AFFIRMATION OF THE MONTH

There is power in my vulnerability, and I show both courage and strength when I show it

NOV 27 – DEC 3
VULNERABILITY

27 / MONDAY ○	28 / TUESDAY	29 / WEDNESDAY

NOTES

> "We are constantly incited to be who we are."

HENRY DAVID THOREAU (1817–1862), AMERICAN WRITER AND PHILOSOPHER

30 / THURSDAY
St Andrew's Day

1 / FRIDAY
World AIDS Day

2 / SATURDAY

3 / SUNDAY
First Sunday of Advent

SMALL ACTS OF VULNERABILITY

Being emotionally vulnerable doesn't always
have to involve big, soul-searching gestures.
Sometimes small acts of vulnerability can mean
a lot, such as letting someone know just how
much you appreciate all that they do for you.

DEC 4 – DEC 10
VULNERABILITY

4 / MONDAY	5 / TUESDAY ☾	6 / WEDNESDAY

NOTES

> "Vulnerability is not weakness; it's our most accurate measure of courage."

BRENÉ BROWN (1965–PRESENT), AMERICAN PROFESSOR AND AUTHOR

7 / THURSDAY
Hanukkah begins at sundown

8 / FRIDAY
Bodhi Day (Buddha's Enlightenment) in some countries

9 / SATURDAY

10 / SUNDAY

SHOW YOUR TRUE SELF

This week, think about a time when you showed someone your vulnerable side. Did you find it easy? How did the interaction affect your relationship with this person? Write down your thoughts and commend yourself for having had the courage to show your true self, scars and all.

DEC 11 – DEC 17
Vulnerability

11 / MONDAY	12 / TUESDAY ●	13 / WEDNESDAY

NOTES

> "The weak can never forgive.
> Forgiveness is the attribute of the strong."

MAHATMA GANDHI (1869–1948), INDIAN LAWYER, ACTIVIST AND LEADER

14 / THURSDAY

15 / FRIDAY

16 / SATURDAY

17 / SUNDAY

FORGIVE YOURSELF

We often stubbornly hold on to things that it would be more useful to get brave, get vulnerable and forgive ourselves for. With this in mind, take a moment to complete this sentence in whatever way feels appropriate for you: "I forgive myself for ...".If needs be, say it over and over again until you begin to believe it.

18 / MONDAY	19 / TUESDAY ☽	20 / WEDNESDAY

NOTES

> "Be yourself; everyone else is already taken ..."
>
> OSCAR WILDE (1854–1900), IRISH POET AND PLAYWRIGHT

21 / THURSDAY ♑

22 / FRIDAY
Winter Solstice (UK, ROI, CAN, USA)
Summer Solstice (AUS, NZ)

23 / SATURDAY

24 / SUNDAY
Christmas Eve

SPEAK YOUR TRUTH

Our desire to be accepted by others often overrides our capacity to speak our truth. Think of a time when you purposefully held something back due to fear of rejection. How did this feel? Have there been times when you've felt more comfortable to be honest about the same thing? How did this feel in contrast?

DEC 25 – DEC 31
vulnerability

25 / MONDAY
Christmas Day

26 / TUESDAY
Boxing Day
St Stephen's Day
Kwanzaa begins

27 / WEDNESDAY ○

NOTES

> "Always be a little kinder than necessary."

J. M. BARRIE (1860–1937), SCOTTISH NOVELIST AND PLAYWRIGHT

28 / THURSDAY

29 / FRIDAY

30 / SATURDAY

---

31 / SUNDAY
New Year's Eve

ENCOURAGE OTHERS TO OPEN UP

Often when we ask, "How are you?", we leave it at that. What would happen if you followed it up with "How are you *really*?" Try this with someone this week and see what happens. Although only a small gesture, it might just create the little bit of space they need to open up and show their more vulnerable side.

DECEMBER OVERVIEW

M	TU	W	TH	F	SA	SU
27	28	29	30	1	2	3
4	5	6	7	8	9	10
11	12	13	14	15	16	17
18	19	20	21	22	23	24
25	26	27	28	29	30	31

This month I am grateful for . . .

_____
_____
_____
_____
_____
_____
_____

REFLECTIONS ON VULNERABILITY

How have you sought to share your truth more this month, thereby opening the door of vulnerability?

How has being more open to showing your vulnerable side felt for you?

Can you see the strengths in being more honest and vulnerable moving forward?

INSPIRED JOURNALLING

The journalling pages that follow will encourage you to spend a little time reflecting on some of the fundamentals in life, which I hope will help you to enjoy a happy, fulfilling year.

Each of the six pages corresponds to one of the monthly themes in the main diary and gives you space to create a personalized list or summary – of ways to bring more comfort into your life, reasons to trust yourself, reminders of when you've shown fortitude in life, activities that help you relax, places that you'd like to visit and times when you have felt truly "heard" and valued in life.

Feel free to write down as few or as many ideas as come into your mind under each theme – there's no right or wrong here. And remember that you can come back to these lists and add to them any time you want. You can also continue them elsewhere if you'd like. So just use them as will best benefit you...

Things That Bring Me Comfort

COMFORT (MARCH)

Knowing – and therefore being able to tap into – what we find comforting in times of stress can really help us to maintain and develop emotional wellbeing. Taking the time to get to know your own healthy coping mechanisms and ways of self-soothing is therefore a valuable thing to do.

When you're in need of some comfort and reassurance, do you know what works for you? Use this space to write down anything that helps you in times of difficulty – a "Comfort List", if you like. This could include anything from taking a walk, watching TV, crafting or reading, to having a nice warm bath, calling a loved one, having a duvet day or getting an early night. Then refer back to this list any time you need some comforting ideas.

A PEP TALK

TRUST (JULY)

We humans can be our own harshest critics at times – and therefore our own worst enemies. Battling with our never-ending worries, perceived limitations and internal negative voices can really leave us feeling drained and without much belief in ourselves at all. One way to challenge such negative thought patterns is by writing some confidence-boosting, trust-enhancing words about ourselves.

Use the space below to write yourself a little pep talk. There's no need to be self-deprecating here. This is a place to really go for it and sing your own praises. What makes you the fantastic person that you are? What have you done that highlights your best qualities? Write it all down here so that you have a reminder to turn to when you're next having a tough day and need an injection of self-belief.

Tip: If you find it difficult writing positive, trust-building things about yourself, pretend you are writing about a friend instead – and let the kind words flow.

Times I Have shown Fortitude

FORTITUDE (AUGUST)

Let's face it – we humans make it through every difficult experience in life thanks to our strength of spirit and fortitude. So taking a little time to pause, reflect and congratulate yourself on all you've come through up until now can be a wonderful way of upping your confidence and preparing yourself for whatever life has in store for you next.

With this in mind, take a moment to think about all the times that your fortitude has got you through something challenging – and write them down below. This can be absolutely anything, no matter how big or small – exams, break-ups, house moves, job moves, arguments with friends, divorce, bereavement – anything goes! You can then refer back to this list if ever you need a reminder of how amazingly strong you are at the core.

_____

_____

_____

_____

_____

_____

_____

_____

_____

_____

_____

what Helps Me to Relax

REST (SEPTEMBER)

We're often so busy trying to fit everything into our busy lives that relaxation gets pushed to the bottom of the pile. Yet how can we function well if we don't give ourselves a healthy foundation of rest and relaxation on which to do it? And how can we effectively give our time and energy to others if we're running on empty *ourselves*?

Sometimes we get so carried away on the conveyer belt of life's tasks that it can feel hard to even remember what might help us get off and unwind a little. With this in mind, use the space below to make a list of activities that you find relaxing. This can include anything – from cooking, painting, reading or walking, to dancing in your living room! Once you've made the list, refer back to it any time you need a reminder to relax!

Places I'd Love to visit

EVOLVING (OCTOBER)

Experiencing new places is a wonderful – and fun! – way of expanding our outlook and continuing to aid our personal growth and development as we move through life. Getting away somewhere different, exploring a new landscape, meeting new people and immersing ourselves in different cultures and languages or dialects often pushes us out of our comfort zones to wonderful new experiences and connections – expanding our horizons to consider new ways of doing, being, speaking, eating, drinking, dancing and all the rest.

With this in mind, use the space below to make a list of all the places that you'd particularly love to visit – both in your own country and beyond, both cities and countryside, both mountains and seaside. Anywhere at all! Then use this list to refer back to when you are in the position to take some time off or book a trip away.

Times in My Life That I've Felt Truly Heard

LISTENING (NOVEMBER)

Active listening, during which we are mindful of not just the other person's words but also the context in which they are saying them, is a rare and valuable thing. When someone gives you their full, intentional focus – properly taking on board what you're saying and looking to respond with a sense of compassion and caring, rather than simply waiting their turn to speak – a bond of trust is formed in which you can feel truly "heard".

Use the space below to make a list of times that you have felt truly "heard" in this way by people in your life. Who was it that made you feel that way? What did they do (or not do) versus others? And what can you learn from such experiences that you could use to help others feel heard and valued in a similar way?

Notes From the Author

Hello, I'm Jess – a designer, illustrator and writer based in West Yorkshire, UK.

I run my Instagram page @jessrachelsharp, where I share gentle positive reminders for when you might need them most. I also have my own line of stationery, enamel pins and gifts, which I sell from my website: www.jessrachelsharp.com. My hope is that my products can offer some support and encouragement through life's many ups and downs.

I began doing what I do after going through a bit of a tough time and attending therapy. I wanted to remember all the helpful words that I was hearing and life-enhancing epiphanies that I was having, so I began to incorporate them into designs. I started posting them to my Instagram and I realized that not only were they helpful for me, but they resonated with others, too. And I haven't stopped since!

It has been an absolute dream to work with Watkins Publishing on putting these ideas into this diary. I hope you find it as uplifting and inspiring to read and use as I have found it to create.

We are constantly learning and growing on our journey through life, so I hope that this diary can offer some gentle guidance for you along the way – helping you to discover more about yourself and make the very most of each and every day.

Here's wishing you much love, hope and happiness for a fulfilling year ahead!

Jess xxx

Notes